D1288357

21st
Century
Skills Library

REAL WORLD MATH: NATURAL DISASTERS

VOLCANIC ERUPTIONS

BY NANCY ROBINSON MASTERS

Published in the United States of America by
Cherry Lake Publishing, Ann Arbor, Michigan
www.cherrylakepublishing.com

Content Adviser
Jack Williams
Founding editor of the *USA Today* weather page and author of *The AMS Weather Book: The Ultimate Guide to America's Weather*

Math Adviser
Katherine M. Gregory, M.Ed

Credits
Cover and page 1, ©Juliengrondin/Dreamstime.com; page 4, ©Andrea Danti/ Shutterstock, Inc.; page 7, ©Sergio Ponomarev/Shutterstock, Inc.; page 8, ©beboy/ Shutterstock, Inc.; page 10, ©Nilanjan Bhattacharya/Dreamstime.com; page 13, ©Jeff Banke/Shutterstock, Inc.; page 14, ©Johann Helgason/Shutterstock.com, pages 17 and 19, ©AP Photo/Michael Probst; page 20, ©Tristan3D/Shutterstock, Inc.; page 23, ©NASA; page 24, ©Sam DCruz/Shutterstock, Inc.; page 26, ©vicspacewalker/Shutterstock, Inc.; page 28, ©Chmpagndave/Dreamstime.com

Library of Congress Cataloging-in-Publication Data
Masters, Nancy Robinson.
  Volcanic eruptions/by Nancy Robinson Masters.
      p. cm.—(Real world math)
  Includes bibliographical references and index.
  ISBN 978-1-61080-328-1 (lib. bdg.)—ISBN 978-1-61080-337-3 (e-book)—
ISBN 978-1-61080-414-1 (pbk.)
  1. Volcanic eruptions—Juvenile literature. 2. Mathematics—Problems, exercises, etc.—Juvenile literature. I. Title.
  QE522M327 2012
  551.2101513—dc23   2011035045

Cherry Lake Publishing would like to acknowledge
the work of The Partnership for 21st Century Skills.
Please visit *www.21stcenturyskills.org* for more information.

Printed in the United States of America
Corporate Graphics Inc.
January 2012
CLSP10

TABLE OF CONTENTS

CHAPTER ONE
WHAT IS A VOLCANIC ERUPTION?

We live on the **crust** of the earth. The earth's crust is about 18 miles (29 kilometers) thick. Beneath the crust is a layer of rock called the **mantle**, which is around

It is very hot inside Earth's deepest layers.

1,800 miles (2,900 km) thick. Inside the mantle is the earth's **core**. **Magma**, or melted rock, and gas are trapped in the core. A volcanic eruption occurs when magma from deep inside the earth pushes up through the mantle and the crust. Magma that reaches the earth's surface is called **lava**. Steam and gases, such as carbon dioxide, are also released into the atmosphere during a volcanic eruption.

Volcanologists are scientists who study volcanoes. They place volcanoes in three large categories. An **active** volcano has had at least one eruption during the past 10,000 years. A **dormant** volcano has not erupted for some time, but it is expected to erupt again. An **extinct** volcano has not erupted in the past 10,000 years and is not expected to erupt again.

What causes a volcano to erupt? Volcanologists say that eruptions are caused when giant moving slabs of the earth's crust and upper mantle collide or grind against one other. These slabs are called **tectonic plates**. As two tectonic plates collide, pressure squeezes magma up between the plates, causing a volcanic eruption. Volcanoes can also erupt when tectonic plates drift apart.

Some volcanoes erupt because of weak areas in a plate called **hot spots**. The volcanoes of the Hawaiian Islands are examples of eruptions from a hot spot. Hawaii's Mauna Loa is the biggest volcano on earth. It is 60 miles (97 km) long, 30 miles (48 km) wide, and 33,476 feet high (10,203 meters) measured from the bottom of the Pacific Ocean.

Volcanic eruptions can cause fires, mudslides, floods, avalanches, and earthquakes. Lava flows can reach speeds of 90 to 100 miles per hour (145 to 160 kph) as they slide down the side of a volcano. These kinds of eruptions can push down entire forests. They can change the course of rivers. They affect the air we breathe, the food we eat, and the water we drink.

Some eruptions occur suddenly. In 1815, Mount Tambora on the island of Sumbawa, Indonesia, erupted, killing between 70,000 and 90,000 people. The explosion was heard more than

 LIFE & CAREER SKILLS

Volcanologists have a hot job! They study how and why volcanoes erupt. They also gather and measure samples of volcanic ash and gases. They map lava flows and use problem-solving skills to predict when and where future eruptions may happen. Most volcanologists have college degrees. They must have strong skills in math, science, geography, history, biology, chemistry, physics, and computers. They are often called upon to do hands-on fieldwork, so camping, hiking, and observation skills also come in handy. You can find out more about becoming a volcanologist at the American Geological Institute Web site *www.agiweb.org/workforce/careers.html.*

Volcanologists travel around the world to learn more about volcanoes.

1,200 miles (1,930 km) away. Most of the deaths resulted from starvation and disease. The poisonous gas and ash that filled the air and covered the ground made it impossible for crops to grow. Thousands died from a lack of food and clean water.

The massive eruption resulted in climate change in many parts of the world. So much ash and other volcanic material filled the air that it blocked the sunlight, causing a "volcanic winter." Crops failed and livestock died in many parts of the Northern Hemisphere during what became known as the "Year Without a Summer." The eruption of Tambora resulted in the worst famine of the 19th century.

Some eruptions throw lava high into the air.

Not all volcanoes erupt suddenly. In 1943, a farmer saw smoke and heard hissing noises coming from a crack in the ground of his cornfield near Mexico City. For the next 9 years, lava flowed steadily from the crack. The buildup of lava eventually created a volcanic mountain 7,454 feet (2,272 m) high.

A new volcano erupted for the first time on June 4, 2011, in the Andes Mountains of Chile. The eruption created a column of ash 6 miles (10 km) high. The ash spread across South America and the Atlantic Ocean. It reached as far as Melbourne, Australia—more than 7,000 miles (11,265 km) away!

REAL WORLD MATH CHALLENGE

The volcano in Chile first erupted on June 4, 2011. Ash from the volcano reached the Australian island of Tasmania on June 13. If Tasmania and Chile are about 6,000 miles apart, how many miles did the ash cloud travel each day? Write your answer as a mixed number.

(Turn to page 29 for the answer)

CHAPTER TWO

PLOTTING THE POWER OF A VOLCANIC ERUPTION

S cientists plot the power of a volcanic eruption on the Volcanic Explosivity Index (VEI) scale. The VEI is a scale that begins at 0 and goes to 8. Zero is the least explosive, and 8 is the most explosive. The numbers represent the

Mount St. Helens is peaceful most of the time, but it has erupted with incredible force.

amount of volcanic material erupted, how high the material was spewed, and how long the eruption lasted.

A nonexplosive volcano is one that does not erupt with force. It is rated 0 on the VEI scale. Nonexplosive underwater volcanoes are called **seamounts**. About 20 percent of the earth's volcanoes are seamounts.

The deadliest volcanic eruption in U.S. history was from Mount St. Helens in the state of Washington on May 18, 1980. It measured a 5 on the VEI scale. A sudden surge of magma broke through the mantle. Mudflows and avalanches killed 57 people in the volcano's "red zone." The red zone is an area 6 to 10 miles (10 to 16 km) from the center of the eruption. Scientists estimate that at least 7,000 deer, bears, and other wildlife were also killed. The violence of the eruption sent ash spewing out at close to the speed of sound, or 768 miles (1,236 km) per hour.

An eruption of Krakatau in Indonesia in 1883 is rated 6 on the VEI scale. Between 50,000 and 70,000 people were killed. It

REAL WORLD MATH CHALLENGE

The speed of sound is a measure of how fast sound waves travel. Sound waves travel at different speeds through air or through liquid. If the sound of the Krakatau volcano traveled through the air at 720 miles an hour, how far did it travel in 1 minute? How far did the sound travel in 2.8 hours?

(Turn to page 29 for the answers)

LEARNING & INNOVATION SKILLS

Volcanologists do a lot of research to make sure their information is correct. Read the VEI scale numbers on the chart below. Look at the number of volcanic eruptions during the past 10,000 years for each type of volcano. What types of research could you do to make sure this information is correct? Would you use the Internet? Would you read books about volcanoes? Could you ask your teacher to invite a volcanologist to visit your school? What other ways can you think of?

VEI Number	Description	Examples	Occurrences in Last 10,000 Years
0		Kilauea (United States)	Many
1	Nonexplosive	Stromboli (Italy)	Many
2	Small	Galeras (Colombia) Sinabung (Indonesia)	3,477
3	Moderate	Nevado del Ruiz (Colombia) Etna (Italy)	868
4	Moderate to large	Merapi (Indonesia) Grímsvötn (Iceland)	421
5	Large	Vesuvius (Italy) St. Helens (United States)	166
6	Very large	Krakatau (Indonesia) Pinatubo (Philippines)	51
7		Thera (near Greece) Tambora (Indonesia)	5
8		Yellowstone (United States) Toba (Indonesia)	0

Crater Lake in Oregon is a caldera that filled with water after forming.

made the loudest noise ever heard by humans. People more than 2,000 miles (3,219 km) away heard the sound of the explosions.

The most powerful volcanic eruption is an 8 on the VEI scale. Scientists believe there have only been 47 of these enormous eruptions in the earth's history. The last one occurred more than 26 million years ago.

The force of some eruptions can cause the top of a volcano to collapse. If the top of a volcano collapses, it forms a **caldera**, which comes from a Spanish word meaning "kettle." The La Garita Caldera is in the state of Colorado. Scientists believe it was formed about 28 million years ago from an eruption that was 100,000 times more powerful than the most powerful bomb ever built.

CHAPTER THREE

DO THE MATH: ASH OVER ICELAND

"E15 is at it again!" This announcement on a television news broadcast on March 20, 2010, did not come as a surprise to scientists. E15 is the identification scientists use for the Eyjafjallajökull volcano in southern Iceland. The

Scientists were not surprised when Eyjafjallajökull erupted because it had been showing signs of activity.

volcano spreads across 39 acres (15.8 hectares), and it is covered by a glacier. It had been almost 200 years since E15 erupted. But scientists had been observing signs that it was about to erupt again.

What were the signs? First, the slopes of the volcano had swelled. Vibrations from small nearby earthquakes were also felt. Steam and gases from magma began to escape from the ground. Although some volcanoes give only a few hours' warning before they erupt, E15 had shown signs for several months.

REAL WORLD MATH CHALLENGE

Some volcanoes erupt on a regular schedule. Scientists believe that Yellowstone National Park in Wyoming sits on top of a supervolcano that first erupted 2 million years ago. They believe that it has erupted every 700,000 years since. The Eyjafjallajökull volcano in southern Iceland erupted on March 20, 2010. This was the same day it had erupted about 200 years earlier. If a volcano erupted in the year 1055 for the first time and has erupted every 225 years since, how many times has it erupted since 1055? What was the most recent year it erupted? When is the next eruption due if it continues to erupt on schedule?

(Turn to page 29 for the answers)

21ST CENTURY CONTENT

The Global Positioning System (GPS) is an important tool volcanologists use to help reduce danger before and after a volcano erupts. GPS satellites circling the earth send radio signals to receivers on the ground. These signals provide the exact locations of volcanoes. The satellites relay information about the size, shape, and movement of eruptions. They also report bulges that sometimes develop in the sides of volcanoes before they erupt. The bulges are one of the key signals that volcanic observatories watch for. Maps can also be drawn quickly with computers using accurate GPS information. Saving time saves lives when tracking a volcanic eruption.

Finally, on that March day, the volcano erupted. The glacier ice melted, becoming extremely cold water. It mixed with lava, which flowed from the volcano with a temperature of 1,800 degrees Fahrenheit (982 degrees Celsius). The hot lava caused the water to vaporize instantly, with a force that sent a huge column of steam and ash 10 miles (16 km) high into the sky. Volcanic ash is made of tiny pieces of hard,

Smoke and ash clouds from the Eyjafjallajökull eruption were visible from many miles away.

sharp glass. It can ruin the engines of a jet airplane that is in flight. Winds carried the ash from the Eyjafjallajökull eruption into the flight paths used by commercial airliners. More than 100,000 flights had to be canceled during an 8-day period because of this enormous column of ash. The cloud of ash spread over the United Kingdom and Europe. The ash continued to spread for months.

On May 21, 2011, another volcano in southern Iceland erupted. The Grímsvötn volcano sent a column of ash about 7 miles (11 km) above the earth. The Grímsvötn eruption forced 120 million tons of ash into the sky during the first 48 hours it erupted. Eyjafjallajökull and Grímsvötn were both rated 4 on the Volcanic Explosivity Index scale. But Grímsvötn did not receive as much news coverage as E15 did because the eruption lasted only a few days. Fewer flights had to be canceled, and the ash did not spread as far or for as long.

Many people were left stranded in airports when their flights were canceled because of the Eyjafjallajökull eruption.

CHAPTER FOUR

DO THE MATH: OUT-OF-THIS-WORLD ERUPTIONS

E arth is not the only place in our solar system where volcanoes have erupted. Powerful modern telescopes

There are many large volcanoes on Mars.

and photographs taken by unmanned spacecraft show the planet Venus is covered with volcanoes! Some may still be active. Craters caused by volcanic eruptions also cover the planet Mercury. Scientists believe Mercury's volcanoes are extinct like those on Earth's moon.

Volcanoes on Mars are 10 to 100 times larger than those on Earth. The biggest volcano in our solar system is on Mars. Olympus Mons volcano is 90,000 feet high (27,500 m) and in its widest place is 20 times wider than it is high. Its average width is 1,800 feet (550 m). It is close to 193,000 square miles (500,000 sq km) in area. That makes it about the size of the country of Spain or the state of Arizona. Scientists believe Olympus Mons rose from a hot spot like Hawaii's Mauna Loa.

The planet Jupiter does not have volcanoes, but one of Jupiter's two moons does. Jupiter's moon Io may be home to the most active volcanoes in our solar system. Scientists think there have been as many as 500 eruptions on Io in the last 100 years.

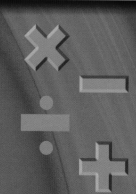

REAL WORLD MATH CHALLENGE

Jupiter's moon Io is home to all types of volcanic activity. Scientists have observed eruptive centers, which are locations of major volcanic activity, as well as depressions in the ground called paterae. Io also has many lava flows. These lava flows are named after fire and thunder gods from various mythologies and cultures. The following chart is a list of seven lava flows on Io. Use the chart to answer the questions below.

Name of Lava Flow	Length of Lava Flow (in kilometers)
Acala (Buddhist)	411
Donar (Germanic)	222
Euboea (Greek)	105
Fjorgynn (Norse)	414
Lei-Kung (Chinese)	386
Masubi (Japanese)	501
Sobo (Vodou)	58

a. What is the total length of the lava flows?
b. What is the difference between the longest lava flow and the shortest?

(Turn to page 29 for the answers)

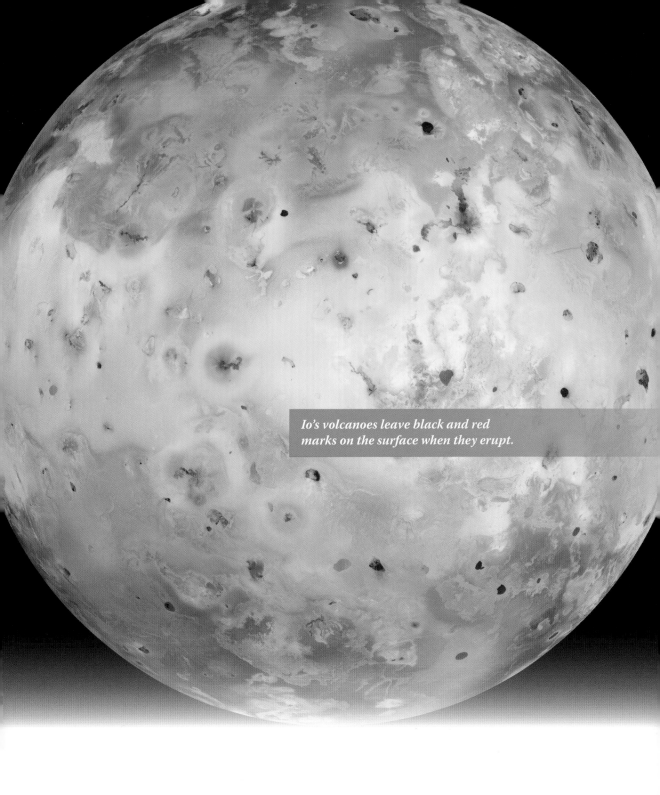

Io's volcanoes leave black and red
marks on the surface when they erupt.

CHAPTER FIVE
COUNT THE BENEFITS

Loss of lives and property make volcanic eruptions among the worst natural disasters on Earth. Volcanoes have killed more than 225,000 people during the past 400 years. The cost of destruction and damage caused by those volcanoes is almost impossible to calculate. The Mount

Volcanoes can be extremely destructive.

St. Helens eruption alone destroyed property worth more than $1 billion. The damage to the environment from eruptions such as Eyjafjallajökull and Grímsvötn may not be known for many years.

Volcanic eruption research costs a lot of money. The United States Geological Survey (USGS) is an agency of the U.S. government that conducts scientific research. The USGS must pay volcanologists to observe and investigate eruptions. It must provide special equipment to measure and record findings. It must also provide tents, clothing, and other supplies scientists need to live and work in remote locations.

REAL WORLD MATH CHALLENGE

Robots have been used to work in areas such as Mount Erebus in Antarctica, the southernmost active volcano on earth. Suppose it costs $3.14 million to operate one robot for one year in Antarctica. It costs $3.14 million for two volcanologists including their equipment to do the same job. The cost of their equipment is $2.12 million. How much does it cost for one volcanologist to work for a year in Antarctica, not including equipment?

(Turn to page 29 for the answer)

Are there any benefits from volcanoes and volcanic eruptions? Yes! They help us learn more about the earth and its history. They provide sources of **geothermal** heat. This underground heat can be used to heat water and to power entire cities. Some volcanic soils are rich in minerals that can help grow rice, vegetables, and fruit crops. These soils can usually produce more than one crop a year.

Pumice rock from volcanic eruptions is used to make building materials such as cement and concrete blocks. Pumice is a very light but coarse rock. It is also used in cleaners, soaps, and cosmetics. Did you use toothpaste this morning? You may have brushed your teeth with toothpaste that had pumice from a volcanic eruption as an ingredient!

Pumice rocks are covered in tiny holes.

Volcanic eruptions can cause huge amounts of destruction. They also help countries work together to have a safer, better world, and we are always learning something new from them. Good or bad, volcanoes are an important part of life on Earth.

LEARNING & INNOVATION SKILLS

Have you ever wanted to build your own volcano? Here's an experiment to try with an adult. You'll need:

Small plastic bottle

Baking soda

Wide tray or baking pan

Sand or dirt

¼ cup of vinegar

Measuring cup with a pouring lip

Red food coloring

- Fill the bottle one-quarter to one-half full of baking soda. Place it in the middle of the tray.
- Pile sand or dirt around the bottle so that you can just see the opening at the top. It should look like a small volcano at this point.
- Pour vinegar into the measuring cup.
- Place several drops of food coloring into the vinegar. Quickly pour it into the bottle.

Stand back and watch your volcano erupt! To find out why your volcano blew its top, research volcano experiments online or at the library.

Making your own volcano can be a lot of fun.

REAL WORLD MATH CHALLENGE ANSWERS

Chapter One

Page 9

The ash travelled $666\frac{2}{3}$ miles each day.

6,000 miles ÷ 9 days = 666.667, or $666\frac{2}{3}$ miles per day.

Chapter Two

Page 11

The sound traveled 12 miles in 1 minute.

720 mph ÷ 60 minutes = 12 miles

The sound traveled 2,016 miles in 2.8 hours.

720 mph × 2.8 hours = 2,016 miles

Chapter Three

Page 15

The volcano has erupted about 4 times since 1055.

2012 (present year) − 1055 = 957 years have passed

957 ÷ 225 = 4.3, or about 4 times

The most recent year it erupted is 1955.

225 × 4 [times it has erupted] = 900 years

1055 + 900 = 1955

The next eruption date is the year 2180.

1955 (most recent year) + 225 years = 2180

Chapter Four

Page 22

a. The total length of lava flows is 2,097 kilometers.

411 + 222 + 105 + 414 + 386 + 501 + 58 = 2,097 total km

b. The difference between the longest and shortest flows is 443 kilometers.

501 (Masubi) − 58 (Sobo) = 443 km

Chapter Five

Page 25

It costs $510,000 for one volcanologist to work for one year.

$3.14 million − $2.12 million (equipment) = $1.02 million, or $1,020,000, for two volcanologists

$1,020,000 ÷ 2 volcanologists = $510,000 for one volcanologist

GLOSSARY

active (AK-tiv) referring to a volcano that has had at least one eruption during the past 10,000 years

caldera (kal-DEHR-uh) a volcanic crater, formed by the collapse of the volcano's top

core (KORE) the intensely hot, most inner part of the earth

crust (KRUHST) the top layer of the earth, made up mostly of rock

dormant (DOR-muhnt) referring to a volcano that has not erupted for some time, but it is expected to erupt again

extinct (ek-STINGKT) referring to a volcano that is not expected to erupt again

geothermal (jee-oh-THUR-muhl) relating to the internal heat of the earth

hot spots (HOT SPOTS) weak spots in a tectonic plate, usually areas of constant volcanic activity

lava (LAH-vuh) the hot, melted rock that pours out of a volcano when it erupts

magma (MAG-muh) melted rock found beneath the earth's surface

mantle (MAN-tuhl) the part of the earth between the crust and the core

seamounts (SEE-mounts) nonexplosive underwater volcanoes

tectonic plates (tek-TON-ik PLATES) huge, thick landmasses that make up the earth's surface

volcanologists (vahl-kuh-nol-uh-jists) scientists who study volcanoes

FOR MORE INFORMATION

BOOKS

Fradin, Judith Bloom, and Dennis B. Fradin. *Volcano! The Icelandic Eruption of 2010 and Other Hot, Smoky, Fierce, and Fiery Mountains*. Washington, DC: National Geographic Children's Books, 2010.

Manatt, Kathleen. *Volcanologist*. Ann Arbor, MI: Cherry Lake Press, 2008.

Marsico, Katie. *Mountains*. Ann Arbor, MI: Cherry Lake Press, 2010.

WEB SITES

Discovery Kids—Volcano Explorer
http://kids.discovery.com/games/build-play/volcano-explorer
Visit this site to learn about why volcanoes erupt, where they're most common, and even try creating your own volcano!

National Park Service—Hawai'i Volcanoes
www.nps.gov/havo/forkids/index.htm
Check out this site for information, videos, and fun activities relating to Hawaii's volcanoes.

INDEX

ABOUT THE AUTHOR

Nancy Robinson Masters is an airplane pilot who traveled to Antarctica as a guest of the National Science Foundation. Seeing Mount Erebus and meeting volcanologists working there are some of her favorite memories! Nancy has written more than 35 books and is a popular visiting author in schools around the world. She lives 13,000 miles from Antarctica in the Elmdale Community near Abilene, Texas, with her husband, veteran aviator Bill Masters. They enjoy flying over West Texas to see where extinct volcanoes erupted. You can get to know her better by visiting her Web site, *http://NancyRobinsonMasters.com*.